To Maggie
Have fun in
Philadelphia!
Elaine A. Kelly
Jean R. Carl
Kathleen Hoover

Copyright © 2009 by Elaine A. Kelly and Jean R. Carl
ISBN 978-0-578-06873-2

All rights reserved. No part of this book may be reproduced or transmitted in any form or by any means, electronic or mechanical, including photocopying, recording, or by any information storage and retrieval system, without permission in writing from the copyright owners.

Printed in the United States of America
First Printing November 2010

AMONG THE BUILDINGS THAT TOUCH THE SKY

PHILADELPHIA

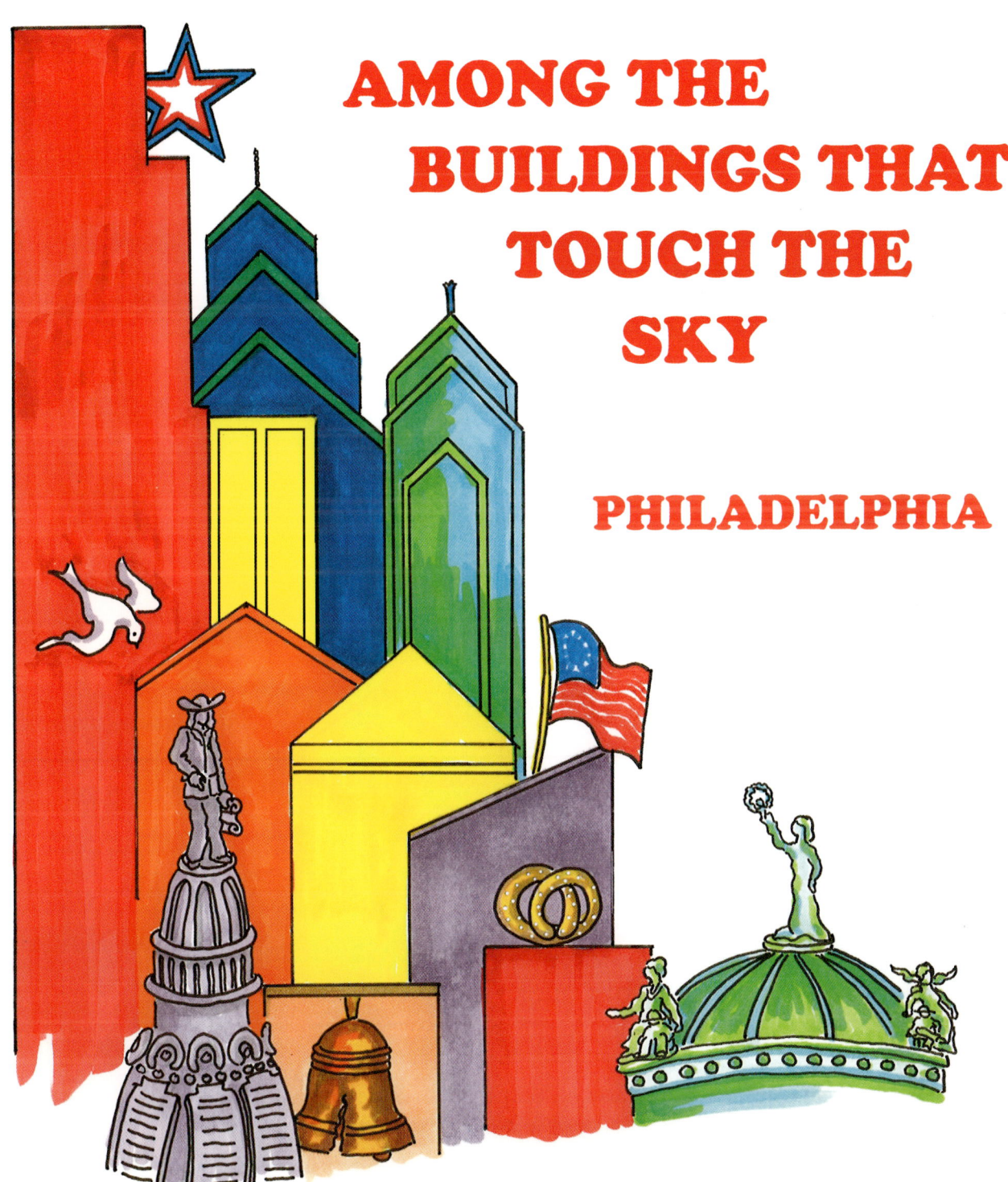

BY ELAINE A. KELLY
AND JEAN R. CARL

ILLUSTRATED BY
CATHLEEN L. NOONE

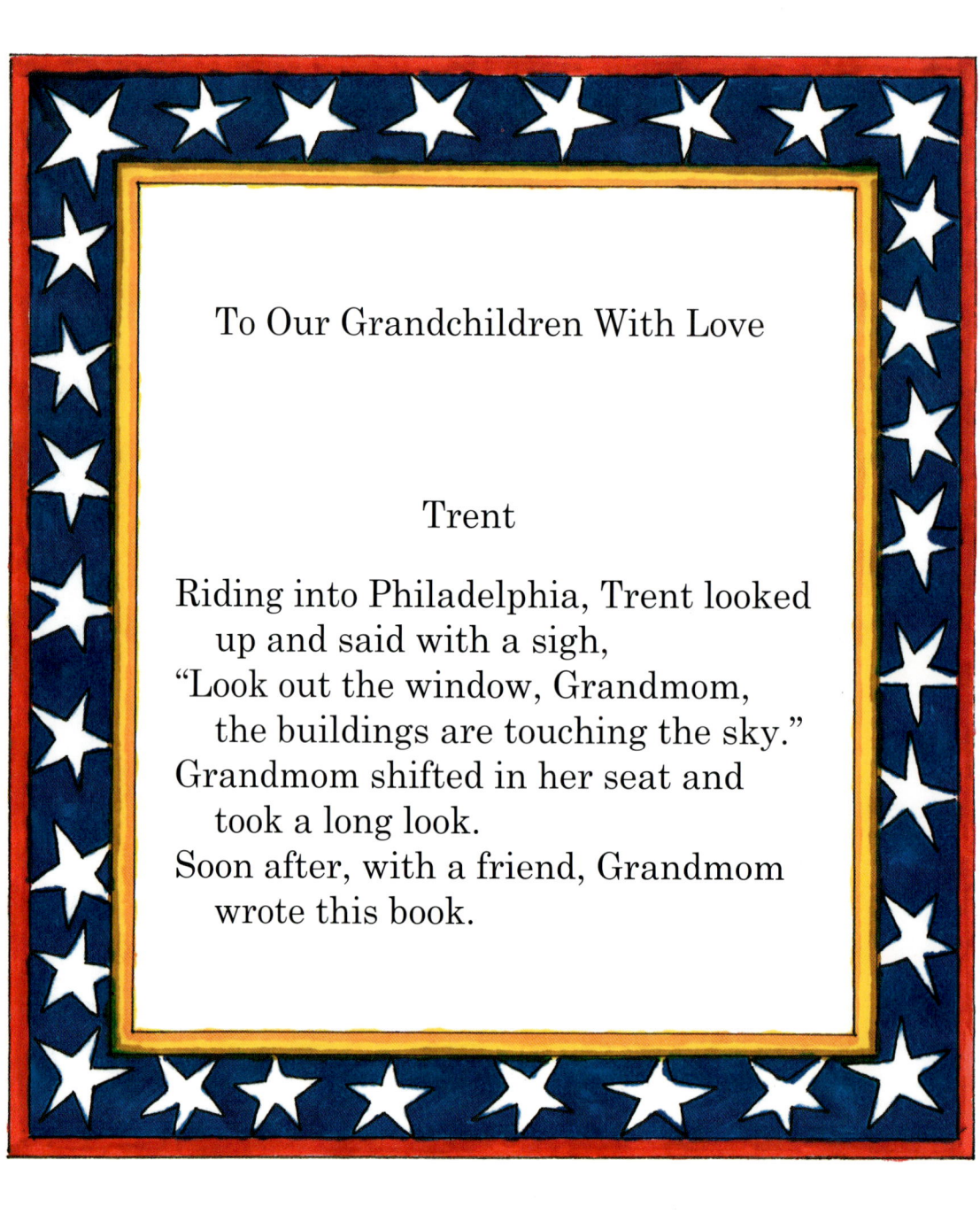

To Our Grandchildren With Love

Trent

Riding into Philadelphia, Trent looked
   up and said with a sigh,
"Look out the window, Grandmom,
   the buildings are touching the sky."
Grandmom shifted in her seat and
   took a long look.
Soon after, with a friend, Grandmom
   wrote this book.

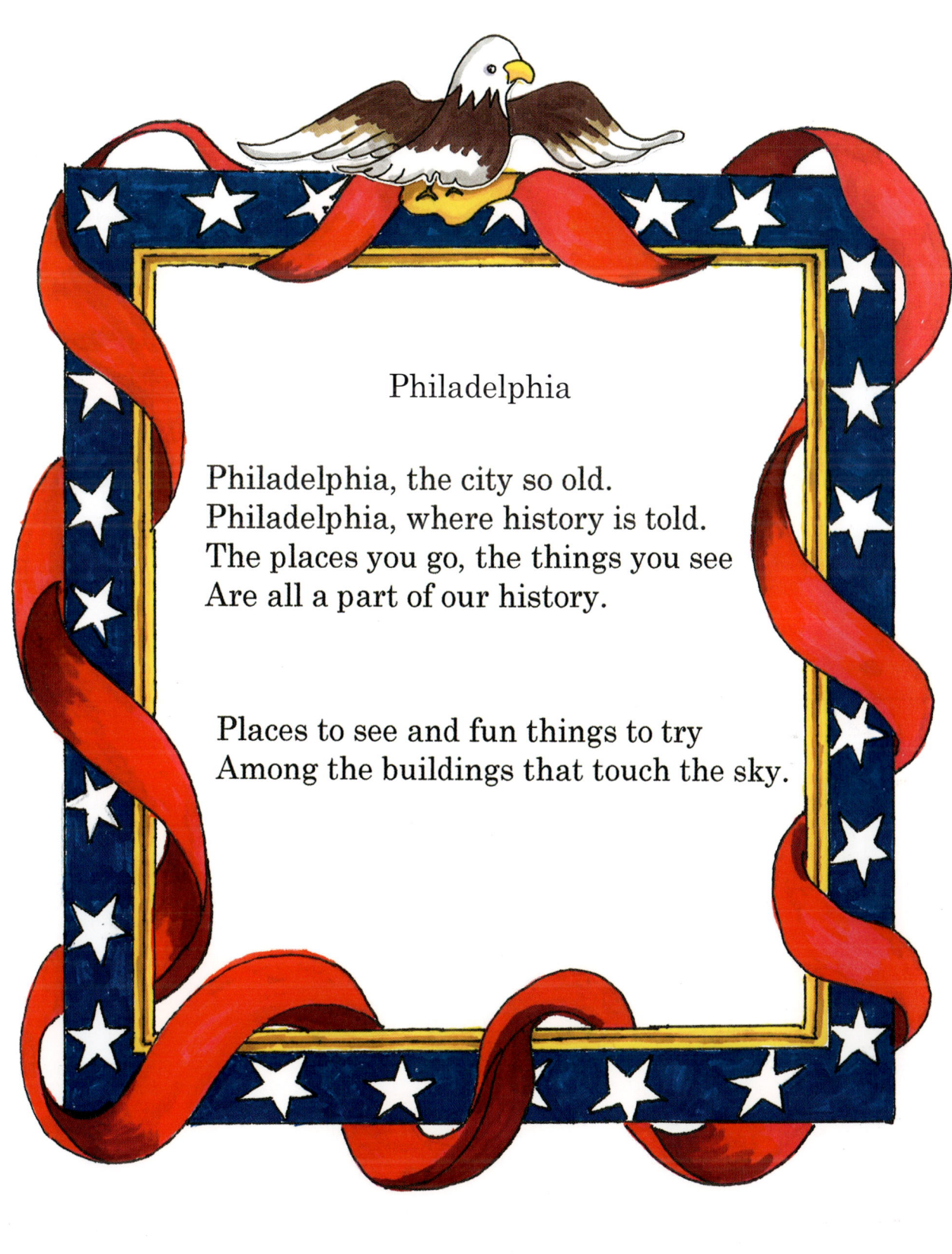

Philadelphia

Philadelphia, the city so old.
Philadelphia, where history is told.
The places you go, the things you see
Are all a part of our history.

Places to see and fun things to try
Among the buildings that touch the sky.

Independence Hall where our country did start,
Important men did play a part.
Declared independence that 4th of July day
That formed our great country, the U.S.A.

The Liberty Bell rang loud and clear
Until a big crack did appear.
Now it stands for all to see,
A symbol of our liberty.

The center is the place to see and hear
Stories about our Constitution that we hold so dear.
Walk among, honor, and touch
Statues of its signers who did so much.

Not a car, not a truck,
It's only a boat that thinks it's a duck.
Use the quackers to make lots of quacks.
Splash into the water and waddle back.

Some people have said that long ago
Betsy Ross our first flag did sew.
Thirteen stars on a field of blue,
Thirteen stripes are on the flag too.

Look at a quarter, nickel, or dime,
And if on it a "P" you find,
The mint right here made this one.
Tour the mint to see how it's done.

Bumpity-bump, clickity-clack,
A horse and carriage goes like that

On cobblestone streets where you might spy
People telling stories of times gone by.

Chief Tamanend
also known as
Tamany
Tamanee
Tamanen
Tamened
Taming
Teinane

Near the river, Chief Tamany stands,
A bird on his shoulder and
 outstretched hand.
He traded with his friend,
 William Penn,
And shared and kept peace
 with all men.

Atop City Hall, William Penn is found.
See his big hat far from the ground.
Go to the observation deck to view
The city he planned all around you.

On a cobblestone street called Elfreth's Alley,
Colonial children laughed and played loudly.
People still live there today.
It's one of the oldest streets in the U.S.A.

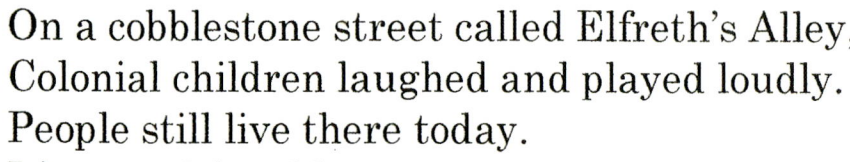

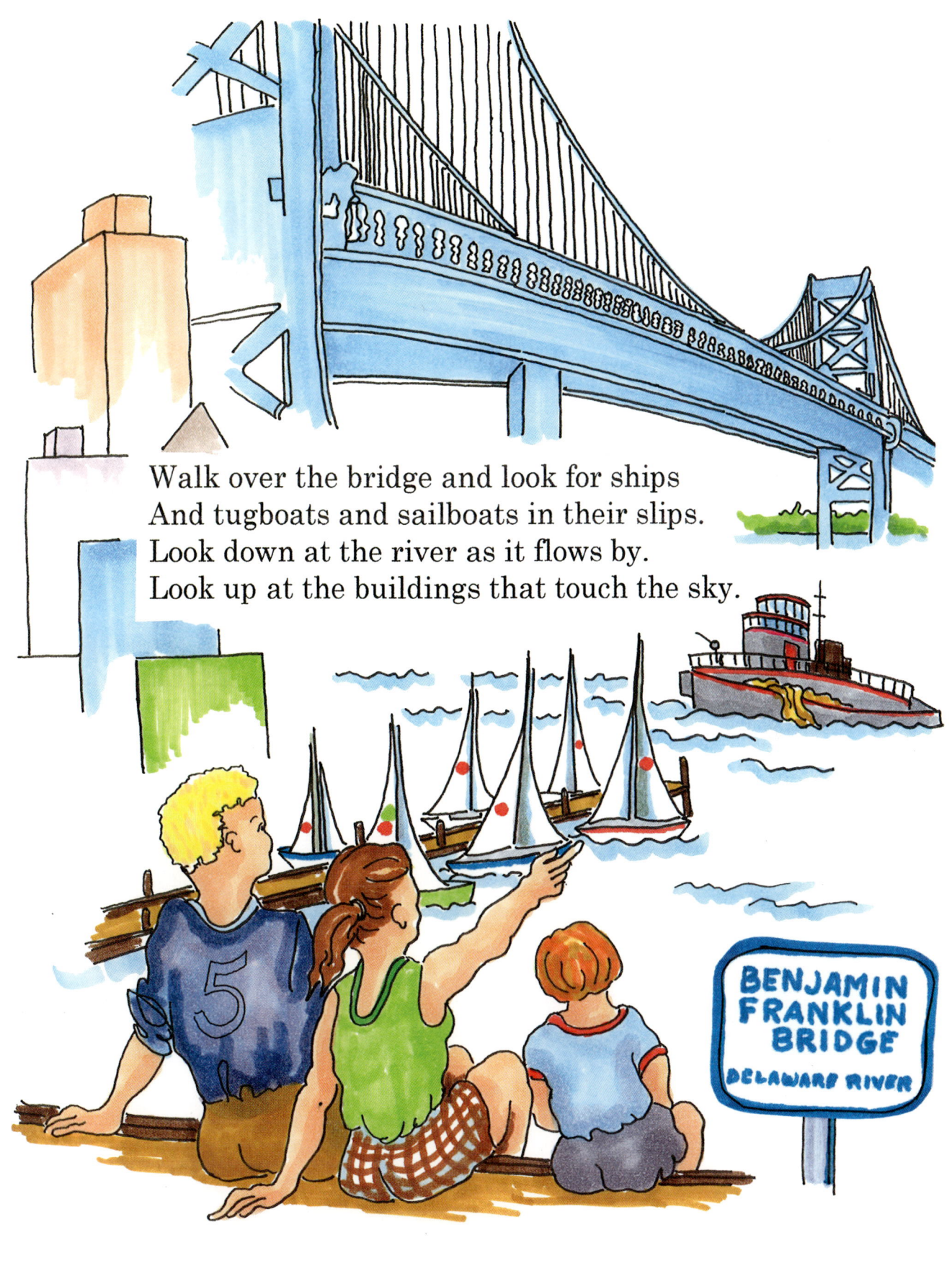

Walk over the bridge and look for ships
And tugboats and sailboats in their slips.
Look down at the river as it flows by.
Look up at the buildings that touch the sky.

Go to Penn's Landing on the Delaware.
Visit the ship museum while you are there.
A cruiser and a submarine, too,
Are there for you to walk through.

IN HONOR OF BENJAMIN FRANKLIN

The institute has lots of parts.
Ride the engine, climb through the heart.
In the planetarium, the stars twinkle bright.
Even in daytime, it looks like night.

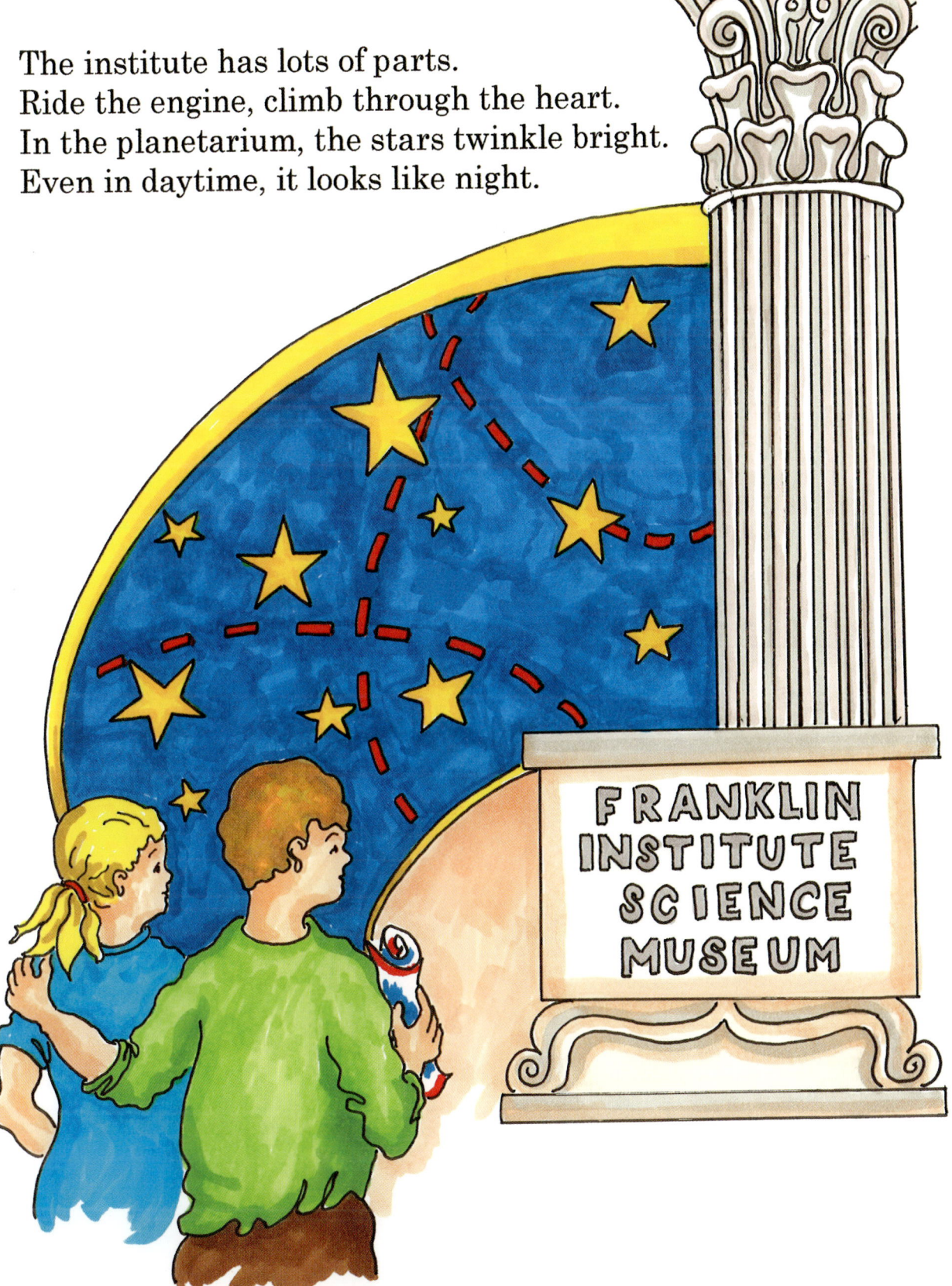

Philly sports fans come to cheer
Their favorite teams that play here.
The arenas can be toured each day
Even when the teams are away.

This museum must be part of your day.
It is here you will want to play.
Fly planes, float boats, ride the carousel.
At the play market, you can buy and sell.

The dinosaur skeleton is huge, it will appear,
In the natural history museum here.
In this building, you will view
Birds, rocks, and butterflies too.

Up, up the steps to reach rooms filled with art.
When you get there, you will start
To see the armor worn by knights
And the pictures with colors so bright.

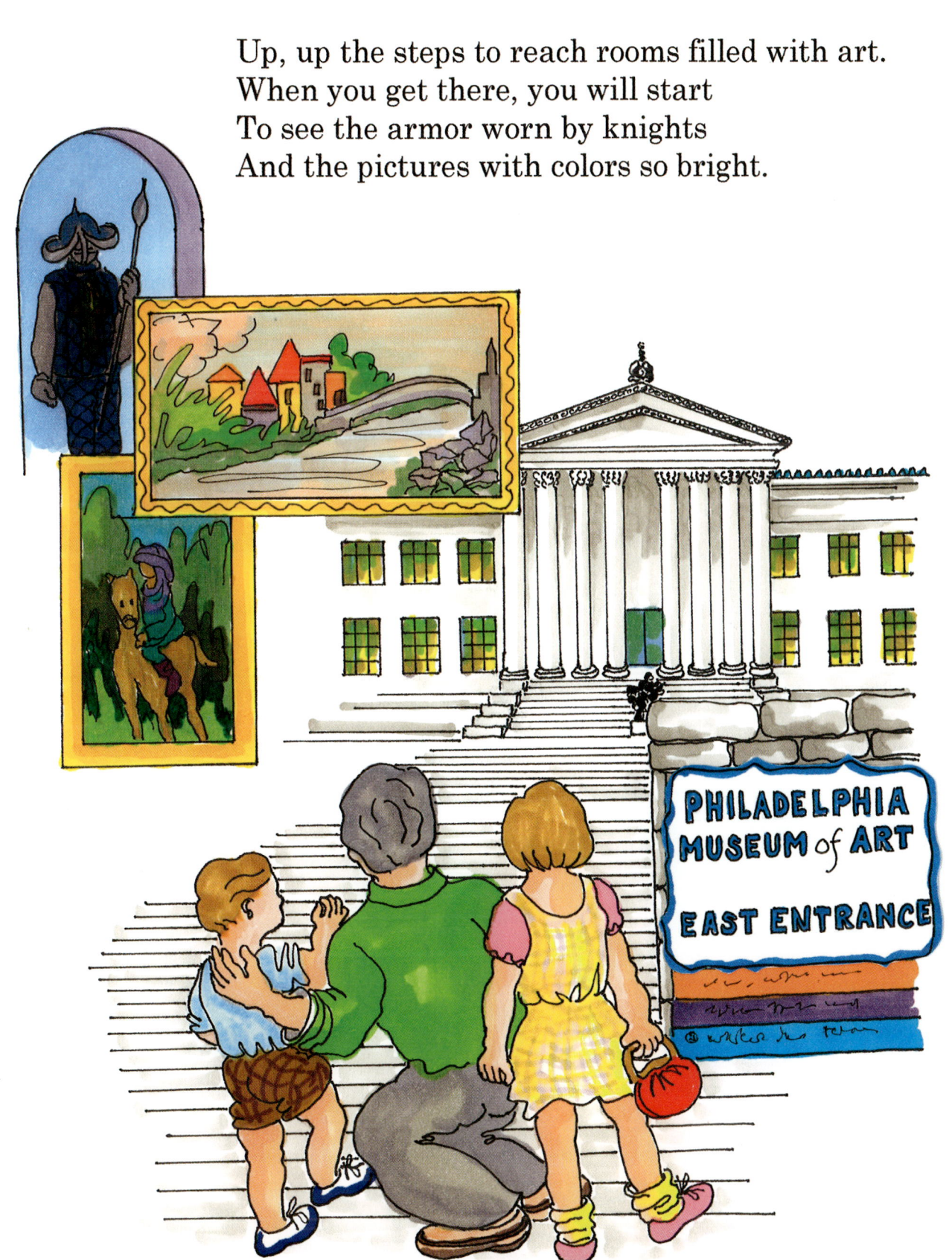

Ride a bus and go to the zoo.
There are giraffes, zebras, and monkeys too.
Camel, pony, or train ride take.
Then paddle a swan boat on the lake.

After a busy day and it's time for a treat,
A soft pretzel or Philly cheesesteak can't be beat.
Then think of everything you've done.
We hope you say "That was fun!"

Places to see and fun things to try
Among the buildings that touch the sky.